Dad's
At
Work

&

Mom
Can't
Drive

Henry J. Grampietro, Jr.

2015

DEDICATION

This book is dedicated to Jack and Bob Zona.

You left us too early.

Also to all the kids that played ball at Ward School Field.

Guy Ferrante	Dominic DiBenedetto
Don Manna	Ken "Lappo" Lapponese
Nello Coppellotti	Mike Davolio
Paul Bianchi	Marty Czarnecki
Mike Caruso	Jay "Charch" Chioda
Bob Aubain	Joe "Busta" Wyman
Ken Largess	Charlie Besardi
Mike D'Errico	Frank Scirploi
Nick Betti	Richie Lysik
Ted Stolaroff	
Joe "Joe Mass" Mastrogiovanni	

CONTENTS

ACKNOWLEDGMENTS

There are certain people I would like to thank for giving me the encouragement to write this book. My wife Debbie, my daughter Kelly, and my son Kevin who were always there for me. Their opinions were very helpful during some tough times. My brother also gave me his valuable moral support.

Another person I would like to thank is my Aunt Josie (Viscardi) Corazzini. She always told me I could do anything I set my mind to. She has been with me every step of the way. The ironic part is, Aunt Josie died almost forty years ago. Also, I would like to thank my Uncle John Zona who would always ask me, "How's the book coming?" Hey Uncle John, it's finally done! And to my son in law David Sommerville for his help in getting this book published.

One last thanks goes to Jim D. While substitute teaching at Assabet Valley Regional High School, I would read different parts to him during my free periods. His input was very important.

INTRODUCTION

Writing this book is a project I've wanted to undertake for a long time. I'm not an author and I don't pretend to be; however, my aim is to bring back the late 1950s and early '60s, as seen through the eyes of an 11-year-old boy.

It was an era of one car families, 15inch black and white TV sets, Gillette Friday night fights, Sunday afternoon rides, and 10-cent Cokes. Girls had names like Kathy, Paula, Debbie, and Mary. Justin, Ryan, or Zack are boy's names you'd hear on the TV westerns. The '50s and early '60s were, for and my friends and me, our innocent years. President Kennedy's assassination, Vietnam, and the Hippie Movement were still years away.

Our world consisted of TV shows such as Howdy Doody, Captain Kangaroo, the Mickey Mouse Club, Leave it to Beaver, and toasting President Eisenhower with a glass of milk on the Big Brother Bob Emery Show.

Conversations mainly centered around baseball. Who was better: Mickey Mantle or Ted Williams? Were you a Red Sox fan or a Yankees fan?

It was a time we didn't have to worry about school shootings, terrorism, internet predators, or strange diseases. Measles, mumps, and chicken pox were childhood illnesses we all seemed to get from time to time.

At five o'clock everyone sat down to supper. We were expected to eat everything that was put in front of us. Nothing was wasted, even if it was broccoli or asparagus. Remember, our parents lived through the Great Depression.

Ice cream was always a special treat. It was our reward for eating everything on our plate. My favorite flavor was always chocolate.

In school, we were expected to be quiet and do our work without question. Heaven help us if our parents were to be called for something we did that didn't please the teacher. Kids were made to repeat a grade for reasons other than not being able to do the assigned work. Teachers were never questioned.

There were no shorts, jeans, or flip flops worn to school. Girls wore skirts and, in many cases, button up blouses. Girls also wore their hair in ponytails. The boys wore slacks, shoes and socks, and a sport shirt. There were no bulky book bags. We carried our books by our side. Girls always carried them in front.

Teachers, at times, and with our parents' full consent, would physically make sure we acted appropriately. As far as our parents were concerned, teachers were always right. They could cause more damage with the stroke of a pen than any other method. I unfortunately, found this out the hard way.

Our neighborhood consisted of bungalow houses closely situated together with very little lawn and very big vegetable gardens. Fruit trees and grapevines were also part of the landscape. It was a neighborhood with a strong Italian American influence. Dominic's or Orlando's were our grocery stores of choice. There we found almost everything we needed from penny candy to fresh meat, and we had to have a note to buy cigarettes for our parents.

Things we think of as standard today would have been a luxury back then. With air conditioning 15-20 years away, we suffered with stifling heat. Fans, open windows, and the local swimming hole kept us cool.

Our house had three bedrooms, one bathroom, and no shower. The big porcelain bathtub served my three uncles well on date night, and me, once a week.

Activities? Baseball was king in those days. Just about all boys played baseball, whether it was Little League, Farm League, or just plain sandlot.

The girls had Girl Scouts or Brownies and weren't allowed to play baseball. They were considered dainty, and playing baseball was a boy's game.

Our Little League was made up of four teams. Because we came from the same section of town, all of us knew each other. This meant that our coaches and managers, who were our fathers, took these games seriously. They hated losing more than we did. The way they yelled, I don't think they could coach today. We knew they didn't mean anything by yelling; it was just their way.

Our mothers were our silent supporters. They would rarely, if ever, venture into their man's baseball world. Mothers were expected to stay home, cook, clean, and be good housewives whether they liked it or not. Their duties at the field included running the snack shack and keeping track of the money.

Race kept a low profile in the early '60s in Shrewsbury, Massachusetts. We didn't speak or even think about it. There was one African American family in town; their sons played on my team, the "Giants." Most of the other "colored kids," as we called them in those days, lived in the inner city. That's the way it was.

For you older readers, this book should bring back some vivid memories. For you younger people, it's a look back at life in the late "50s and early "60s. Was life better back then? Maybe. Are we happier now? I hope so. I know I wouldn't trade growing up in those years for any other time. It was *our* time!

So as the Lone Ranger said, "Return with us now to those thrilling days of yesteryear..."

1 WHY SHREWSBURY?

Shrewsbury, Massachusetts, in the early '50s was considered a bedroom community for the City of Worcester. Incorporated as a town in 1727, it was a large farming community, and with no major waterways running through it, Shrewsbury pretty much stayed that way until the 1800s. At that time, with the Industrial Revolution in full swing and Worcester becoming a manufacturing giant, the early 1900s saw a shift in population. By 1910, many of the immigrants who settled on the east side of Worcester wanted to escape the crowded city life and tenement living. In many cases, as soon as enough money was saved, the natural migration was from the east side of Worcester to the west side or the "Lake Section" of Shrewsbury. Most of these immigrants were Southern Europeans, or more specifically, Italians. Streets like Edgewater Ave, Dewey Road, Baker Ave, and Plainfield Ave were filled with these new arrivals. Almost immediately, the landscape was dotted with huge vegetable gardens, grapevines, and, in many cases, chicken coops. Thus the Lake Section of Shrewsbury was created.

The Edgemere section of town sported a heavy Swedish influence. Names like Larson and Johnson were common in this area. But the main section, or the most dominant section in town, was the Center Section. Settled by the English in the late 1600s and then by the Irish in the mid to late 1800s, the Center had all the clout, political or otherwise. If you lived in this area, you were more likely to be a professional or a farmer.

Blue collar factory workers were the mainstay of the Lake Section. This was the result of the huge manufacturing base that was Worcester. Boston

Turnpike (Route 9), being the main artery through the Lake Section, would make it the perfect location for the immigrants to settle. You see, most of these men didn't drive, which meant buses were their sole means of transportation.

Our house at 15 Baker Ave was the perfect example of this. With its location a stone's throw from Route 9, my grandfather had easy access to the bus route. Baker Ave was a lively and fun street in those days. Summer nights would bring us all out to our porch, or piazza, as we called it back then, to watch all the activity going on around us. In the late '50s, Spag's legendary department store was growing at an amazing rate. My mother always knew someone either entering or exiting the store. Depending on how well we knew them, an invitation would be extended to join us on our porch. You just never knew who would end up there.

Because of Spag's, Baker Ave became the hub of the Lake Section. Other than traveling to Worcester, Spag's was the only reason people from the Center Section would visit our area.

The names of those living on Baker Ave included Garganigo, Robbio, Viscardi, Borghesani, Vesella, Cialone, and Cellucci. On the other side of Route 9, names like Dileo, Cassanelli, Rossi, Pescaro, Copppellotti, and Deterlizzi dominated Edgewater and Plainfield Ave. This was a different world when compared to the center of town.

2 BAKER AVE

If you were to ask anyone over the age of twenty-five, "Do you remember Spag's?" The answering would be a resounding yes.

I lived the first 10 years of my life in a little three-bedroom bungalow approximately two hundred feet from Spag's. My address was 15 Baker Ave. Directly across the street were my great grandparents, the Viscardis. Traveling up Baker Ave on the right were the Borghesanis, Cialones, the Vassellas, and the Carusos. After our house on the left up Baker Avenue came the Giovanellis, the Fulginitis, the Sciascias and the Celluccis. Bordering Route 9 on Baker Ave were the Garganigos. It was quite an ethnic neighborhood, transplanted from Worcester.

In those days, members of our extended family lived with us. As I remember my early years, the house had three bedrooms for seven people. Because my grandmother died many years earlier, I shared a room with my grandfather. That was an experience. My three unmarried uncles slept wherever they could find space.

Built in 1924, the bungalow style house was starting to show its age by the time I came along. Can you imagine a house today with only one bathroom and no shower?

In the kitchen, we had our new Hotpoint refrigerator with a freezer that could barely fit a 10-pound turkey. The washroom was off to the left, complete with a washing machine and squeezedry rollers. There were no dryers that was the clothesline's job. Every yard had clothes hanging on a line.

The parlor, or the living room as they call it today, was made up of two overstuffed chairs and a couch. Rounding out this room was our beautiful 15-inch black and white admiral television set, complete with a V-shaped antenna (that we called "rabbit ears") for better reception.

Smoking was everywhere back then. At various spots in our house, there were small table ashtrays usually filled with old cigarette butts or cigar ashes. The parlor was different. There we had the most beautiful and ornate floor model ashtray. Other than our TV set for entertainment, we would often play records on our mahogany hand-cranked Victrola. Of course, when the music slowed, we'd have to wind it back to normal speed.

There were no cell phones or texting back then. We did have a black table-model dial telephone, which usually was shared with three other parties. That could be a little tricky. Many times, while I was talking on the phone, another party would click in an ask if they could use the phone. This would cut my conversation short.

In my younger years, my great grandparents, who lived directly across the street, housed about 20-25 chickens. At times, with my aunt's assistance, I would go into the chicken coop and quickly snatch the eggs out of the chickens' nests. Those chickens could get pretty nasty, so I had to act fast.

To watch Grampa, as we called him, kill a chicken was really scary. From a squatting position he would calmly call one of the chickens over to him. Grampa would talk to the chicken (in Italian of course), all the time reassuring it that he wouldn't hurt him. As the chicken slowly clawed his way to Grampa, he would gently pick the chicken up and, swiftly as if breaking a pencil, snap its neck. Immediately, he would cut through the neck, causing the body of the chicken to run around in circles. I guess that's where the saying, "You're running around like a chicken with its head cut off" comes from.

After Grampa died in 1957, the chicken coup was taken down and the chickens were gone forever. Now the only chickens I eat come from the supermarket.

Winter snowstorms would usually bring out Spag's brother, Bob, to plow the store's parking lot. This would create huge piles of snow in my front yard. We'd spend all day and into the night sliding down these mountains of white stuff.

Baker Ave today looks very much like an empty movie set. Gone are the Garganigos the Cialones, the Celluccis, the Vasellas, the Viscardis and the Zonas. There is a new shopping plaza planned for Baker Ave, which is supposed to be beautiful, but it will never replace the Baker Ave I remember.

3 HENRY SR..

My parents, Henry and Helen (Zona) Grampietro, were married in St. Anne's Catholic Church on January 15, 1945. My father was on leave from his duties as a Tech 5 engineer during WWII and after a quick honeymoon in Boston, he headed f o r E u r o p e . Upon returning to the states, Dad left his house on Shrewsbury Street, Worcester and moved in with my mother, her father and three brothers in Shrewsbury.

In the Italian American Community, if a guy was 5'7" he was considered tall. Most men's average height was around 5'4" or 5'5". My dad was just about 6 feet tall. Not tall by today's standards, but a giant back then. His huge hands could completely engulf a baseball. Henry Sr. walked in long strides with his size 13 pigeon-toed feet pointing inward. As long as I knew my dad, he had very little hair on top of his head, but fairly thick black hair on the sides. Combine this with my mother being barely 5'2" and a full crop of jet black hair with a widow's peak, they made quite a couple.

My dad and I went everywhere together. It could be a movie, bowling, or one of many sporting events! It was always somewhere different, but always fun. Most of the time he would take not just me, but usually two cousins and a couple of my friends as well.

There was this one particular time we went to a track meet at the Boston Garden. As the contestants were lining up for the 40 yard dash, I noticed one of the sprinters was bald just like my dad. I remember his name, Daryl Newman. When Newman won the sprint, I turned to my dad and said, "Wow, the bald headed guy won the race." Dad looked at me and said, "Why are you surprised? You don't run with your hair." That was my dad. He had a simple answer for everything.

Another time, as my parents were getting ready to go to a wedding, my father's necktie didn't satisfy my mother. She boldly asked, "You're not going to the wedding wearing that tie, are you?" As my dad looked down at my diminutive mother, he replied in question, "Do you think they'll stop the wedding because I'm not wearin' the right tie?"

In 1960 the newly organized American Football League was running a promotion with CocaCola. It consisted of matching bottle caps, with various AFL players' names on the inside, with the proper spot on 2-foot by 2-foot sheets of paper. If you filled 4 sheets you'd receive a genuine, white lined AFL Football. To actually accomplish this, about 16 cases of Coke would have to be consumed, which was almost an impossible task. But my dad had a plan. Since he knew the CocaCola delivery man at his shop, and remembered the guy owed him a favor, it wasn't long before we had four or five full bags of CocaCola bottle caps on our kitchen table. I thought, "Now, what do we do with them?"

Again, Dad had a plan. We would match the correct cap with the corresponding picture on the sheet. Four or five hours were spent accomplishing this task. The key to this was setting it right. As one sheet was finished it would be laid out on the kitchen table with subsequent sheets stacked on top. We didn't glue the caps the first time around. Dad felt we had to make sure all the caps were in the correct s p a c e s. This b e i n g a Friday evening, gluing the caps would come Saturday afternoon. You see, I had a paper route which required my collecting money on Saturday morning. This took priority. I knew those four stacked sheets of bottle caps would be waiting for me when I got home. Little did I realize what I would walk into once I opened that door from the garage that led to our kitchen.

I excitedly walked up those five steps, opened the door and witnessed my mother and three year old brother crawling under the kitchen table picking up bottle caps. As I surveyed the rest of the room, I noticed bottle caps in the sink, on the hutch, on top of the refrigerator and various other places. The bottle cap sheets were lying motionless on the floor. I was absolutely stunned! I quickly asked Mom, "What happened?" She answered disgustingly, "He's sick!," she said. I assumed she meant my dad. I then asked, "Where's Dad?" Without looking up she pointed with her left index finger toward the den.

I quickly turned and found my dad sitting quietly watching TV. I asked him, "What happened? Why are all the bottle caps all over the floor?" His answer was, "I tried to move the sheets and caps off the kitchen table to a counter top. Mom said no. I tried to move them onto the hutch. She said no. I finally asked her, 'Where do you want me to put them?' She replied, 'I don't care, just get them outta here!' She got me so mad I threw everything up in the air." That was my father.

A few days later Dad and I finally did put the bottle caps back on the sheets, but this time they were glued. Dad took the completed sheets to the CocaCola Company and I got my genuine American Football League white lined football. I was the envy of the neighborhood! That football is long gone now, as are Mom and Dad, but I'll never forget the sight of those bottle caps thrown all over the kitchen.

4 THREE TV CHANNELS

Television was very different in the '50s as opposed to today. The kids of today would be amazed at the 12-inch black and white picture tube we, as children, stared at for hours. Today we live in the high-technology age, with new products popping up almost every day.

Television was first shown to the public at the New York World's Fair of 1939. With WWII just around the corner, TV was put in the background.

In the years following the war, Americans had money and were willing to spend it. Automobiles, appliances, and TV sets were now available in limited numbers. People rushed to stores to buy these new picture machines and they'd pay almost anything within reason to be able to say, "I've got a TV set." The neighborhood would be invited to their house to see what little programming was available. It didn't matter; it was television! The eighth wonder of the world.

We got our first TV set in 1951. Having been born in 1949, I don't remember life without television. Why would I? I was barely two years old, but I do recall some of the early programs. We watched shows such as Pinky Lee; Kukla, Fran and Ollie; Ding Dong School, and, at lunch time, we couldn't miss Big Brother Bob Emery.

Big Brother Bob Emery was on WBZ Channel 4 at noon every day. He had white hair, wore black rimmed glasses, and strummed his theme song on the ukulele. Big Brother always referred to us as "Small Fry." At about 12:15 we, along with Big Brother, would raise a glass of milk and give a toast to the President of the United States.

The President at that time was Dwight Eisenhower. I even remember the show's sponsor. It was United Farmers Dairy. Some things I never forget.

TV programming usually started at 6 a.m. At about 5:30 the blank screen would be replaced by a round circle that looked something like a bull's eye. It was called a *test pattern*. We would stare at that test pattern until the low volume humming would stop. This meant the programming would begin, usually *Morning Prayer* followed by some TV show we couldn't care less about. It didn't matter, it was still television. Six thirty would bring the first of the Saturday morning TV programs, starting with Rex Trailer and *Boomtown*.

On a typical Saturday morning, the TV lineup would be shows such as: *Roy Rogers, Fury, My Friend Flicka, Sky King* and the *Lone Ranger*. In the afternoon, we might see pro wrestling, roller derby, or a Red Sox game. Westerns were very popular in the '50s. The evening would bring programs like *Wyatt Earp, Maverick, Cheyenne, Wagon Train*, and *Have Gun will Trave*l with Richard Boone. Having only one TV, we watched what Dad watched. I memorized every western theme on TV.

Situation comedies were very popular also. We laughed at the *Honeymooners*, Milton Berle's *Texaco Star Theatre*, the *Dick Van Dyke Show*, the *Andy Griffith Show*, and *You'll Never Get Rich*, the army show with Phil Silvers.

You see, in those days we had only three channels. Today we might have anywhere from 150 to 200. Every channel comes in bright and clear today. This wasn't the case back then. If you turned on Channel 4, you hoped it wasn't snowy or blurry. There was no cable TV or satellite dish. To get good reception, an aluminum antenna was perched at the highest point on the roof of our house. Once in a while, as we would be watching a program, for no reason the TV picture would start to flip. If this happened, my dad would get up from his overstuffed chair and fiddle with knobs on the front of the TV. He would no sooner correct the problem and get back to his comfortable chair, when the picture would flip again. This could be very aggravating. There were times I'd have to literally stand beside the TV and stop the picture from flipping.

The TV sets of the '50s were constantly breaking down. In the middle of a show, the picture would turn into gray horizontal lines and, with only one TV, we were sunk. My dad would immediately get on the phone and call the TV repair man.

The TV repair man was almost like a doctor in those days. He made house calls with a big black case that double opened from the top. He would calmly turn the TV so the back was facing him, look at the many vacuum tubes, take one out, show it to us and say, "There's the problem." The tube would be blackened. The TV man would then reach into his bag and pull out a little rectangular box. In it was the new tube. After snapping it back into the TV set, we had our television back.

At 12:30 a.m., after Channel 5 news and the *Tonight Show* with Jack Paar, TV would then leave the air. The last image we'd see was the American flag waving, and the *Star Spangled Banner* would be playing. Then there was just static; TV was done for the day. That was television in the 19'50s.

5 WHITE CITY AMUSEMENT PARK & SPAGS

White City Amusement Park was built in 1905 by a wealthy businessman named Horace Bigelow. While attending the Chicago World's Fair of 1898 and seeing the great electric light display, Bigelow decided to string his brand new amusement park with these newfangled lights. Appropriately enough, he called it "White City."

Nestled between Worcester and Shrewsbury, and rimming Lake Quinsigamond, White City was our "vacation spot." The park opened on Memorial Day, had fireworks on the Fourth of July, and closed for the season on Labor Day. It boasted a huge roller coaster, which some said was the highest in the east; a merry-go-round, which we called the "hobbie horses"; a Ferris wheel, shooting galleries and, if for those who had the nerve, the Rocket ships

The Rocket ships were pointed silver cylinders hanging from extended cables. Each held about eight people and had no seatbelts. As the ride started, centrifugal force would extend the ship out over the lake. Luckily, no one ever got hurt, but I often wondered what would happen if those cables ever let go. We would've had one heck of a ride.

Another favorite ride of mine was the Caterpillar. It was kind of a mini-roller coaster. Once the ride started, a canvas canopy would ascend over our heads. Imagine riding a roller coaster in the dark. That was the Caterpillar.

And of course, there were the bumper cars, which I loved. We called them the "Dodge 'Ems". They were little two seat cars that ran on electricity.

The idea was to drive these minicars and avoid getting smashed into by other cars. The fun was to crash into each other. I once hit another car so hard that I got knocked out of the car seat and onto the shiny, metal floor.

The fun house was another attraction at White City. Inside the building was a 12-15 foot wood slatted slide with a small rise at end. To coast down this runway, a burlap bag was necessary and supplied by the park. The bag would prevent us from getting floor burns. But, as expected, the temptation to touch that wood on the way down was too great to pass up. We were all too eager to show the other kids our burns.

In its day, White City hosted many big name celebrities such as Frankie Avalon, Connie Francis and Bobby Darin. My grandfather even told me that the heavyweight champion of the world at the time, Jack Dempsey, made an appearance there. You have to remember, there were no parks like Six Flags or Disney World back in the '50s.

White City Amusement Park closed forever after running its last rides on Labor Day Weekend 1960. This was shortly after my 11th birthday. In its place today is a shopping center, appropriately named White City Shopping Plaza.

Since the park's closing, the town has more than doubled in population. Little do these newer arrivals realize the fun we had or what was on the grounds of the shopping plaza. The days of fun and laughter are forever gone at White City, but in my mind I'll never forget the sights and smells of the park. To this day, whenever I smell or taste cotton candy, my mind immediately drifts back to the rides like the Whip, the Bug and the rocket ships. It was truly the end of an era.
I wish the kids of today could experience the true White City. It was a major part of our lives and the time.

Spag's was originally a trucking garage that was converted into a department store. Unlike its high class cousins in Worcester, such as W.T. Grant or F.W. Woolworth, Spag's was the workingman's department store. It was truly a shopper's paradise. Once there, you'd be overwhelmed by an inventory that would include anything from plumbing supplies to house wares to kids' toys.

There were many different departments in Spag's. My personal favorite was 'The Ramp'. The Ramp was strategically situated in the middle of the store. Upon entering from the Baker Ave side, I'd see it: my Fantasy Land.

Starting from one end of The Ramp to the other, stacked about six feet high, were the most beautiful baseball gloves I'd ever seen. It was to me, an 11-yearold, a mountain of joy. Gloves, w i t h brand names like Wilson and Spaulding, had major leaguers' signatures on them. That meant the big leaguers actually used gloves like these, or so I thought. Usually, on the inside heel of the glove, the price was written in magic marker.

One by one, my friends and I would search for that perfect baseball glove. If we found one, not only did it have to fit, but it had to have the right player's name on it. I wanted a Ted Williams, Frank Malzone or a Jackie Jensen glove. Those were rare. We were more likely to get a Chuck Stobbs or Billy Consolo. Even if I did happen to find the perfect glove, there's no way my father would spend $8.50 to buy it. He'd always ask, "What's wrong with your old glove?"

Lining The Ramp were barrels filled with beautifully carved Hillerich and Bradsby baseball bats. Made of Northern White Ash, they felt like they were made for our hands. The bats came in sizes ranging from 29 to 33 inches in length. To have one of these with a stamped signature of a major leaguer made you very popular at Ward School Field. The drawback was that everybody wanted to use it, which could result in a cracked bat.

Sadly, Spag's, the retail empire that Anthony Borgatti built more than 70 years ago, is now gone. All that's left are empty buildings and, as of this writing, they are slated for demolition. But my memories of The Ramp, as an 11-year-old, will live in my memory forever. I never did get that Ted Williams baseball glove, but I did get a Chuck Stobbs mitt.

---

* Legend has it that when Anthony Borgatti was a boy he liked spaghetti so much his mother nicknamed him Spag. The rest is history.

6 WARD SCHOOL FIELD

Behind Spag's, on Harrington Ave, was a seven room bungalow school house called the General Artemus Ward School, built to honor the first general in the Revolutionary War and to accommodate the rising number of Italian families moving into the area. Interestingly, in the Shrewsbury Town Report of 1920, a request for more books in the Italian language was made for Ward School.

As with any other school, there must be a playground and Ward School was no exception. Sandwiched between Baker Avenue and Harrington Ave was our "Fenway Park." Ward School Field was a little bandbox field with enough rocks to fill a good-sized dump truck. That didn't matter to us, and all that did matter was that it was "our field."

Baseball, to us kids, was everything back then. You didn't ask if you were Catholic or Protestant. You asked if you were a Red Sox or Yankees fan. A sizable part of our neighborhood was dotted with Yankees fans, which made for some good natured arguments. It always seemed like the Yankees fans got the better of it.

Summer mornings would start very early with me getting on my one-speed Columbia bike. All of us had Columbia bikes those days. Some of the kids had three speed English Racer bikes that my parents couldn't afford. Whatever we had, it was better than walking. I would head up to the field about 8 am with my Chuck Stobbs baseball glove dangling from the front handlebars. As I approached the field, inevitably one of my buddies would be without his bike for whatever reason. I'd throw his glove beside mine on the handlebars and he'd jump onto the metal crossbars with his feet hanging idly in the air. It wasn't the most comfortable ride but, again, whatever we had was better than walking.

At the field, the kids that were already there warmed up by playing catch or pepper. Pepper is a game where you have three or four fielders and one batter. The fielders stand 10-12 feet from the batter. As the ball is tossed gently toward him, he bats it back to the fielders. With a shortage of baseballs, it was a nice warm-up. If a kid brought a baseball to the field, he was treated like royalty. The newer the ball, the better he was treated. Also, no matter how bad a player he was, he had to be picked. It was his ball! It was as simple as that.

Bats, on the other hand, were made of wood back then. This meant they cracked or split on a regular basis. Electrical tape or a screw in the bat's handle would remedy that for a little while — at least until the next solid hit.

At the beginning of every game, we would quickly call out the name of our favorite major leaguer. I would immediately scream out "I'm Frank Malzone!" If someone else called him before I did an alternate major leaguer would be selected. It was usually Don Buddin or Pete Runnels. I'd never call out a Yankee name!

Umpires were nonexistent in our games. We made our own calls. On close plays, usually whoever argues the loudest got the call. In sandlot baseball "courtesy," this meant the next close call went the other way. "You owed us one," was the policy.

The end of the game brought us to a favorite part of the day. Most of us went to Dominic's, a little Italian American grocery store owned by Dominic Longo and his wife, Rosie. Win or lose, a walk over to Dominic's was a treat. We couldn't wait to give him a shiny dime for a glass bottle of Pepsi. After playing baseball for two hours in dirt and dust, that Pepsi really hit the spot. Rosie would always get a little testy with us and would try to hurry us along. She would say, "Come ahna chickie." This could mean the difference between getting a squirrel nut or a licorice stick. When selecting candy, we couldn't be rushed. Dominic's always had great ice cream. As you walked through the door, on the right were the gray ice cream freezers. My favorite flavor was always chocolate. There was no such things as sprinkles or any kind of toppings. You got just plain chocolate. All ice cream was served in a cone. The idea was to lick where the bottom of the ice cream meets the top of the cone. His would eliminate any dripping onto your hands. It was kind of a challenge.

Once I decided which flavor I wanted, Dominic would lean down, open the white doors, and scoop out my selection. Onthe edge of that bin was a glass pitcher of water. This was used to clean the scoop of any left over ice cream from the previous sale. I don't think that water was changed all day. That's probably why it turned brown so quickly.

Dominic's lasted until about 1968. The story is that after the store was broken into and Dominic was struck on the head, he closed the store and moved back to Italy. Today, the former Longo Market is an apartment house, which is slated for demolition. If you look closely, you can still see the cement slab we'd step on to enter the store. I can visit Dominic's anytime in my mind.

7 THE BARBERSHOP

In small town America the barbershop is the local hangout. You can always hear the latest news there. It was the Facebook of its day. In 19'50s Shrewsbury, "Joe the Barber's" was that place. It was located on Boston Turnpike almost across from St. Anne's Church and a quarter-mile mile west of Spag's. Formerly D'Errico's Italian American grocery store, it had room for about 12-15 customers.

The original barbershop was across the Lake Quinsigamond bridge into Worcester. It was a little bandbox shop with two barber chairs and a waiting area for about six to eight people. It was always pretty boring waiting for my turn to get my hair cut.

This one particular day when my father got home from work, he decided we should get haircuts. Instead of playing ball with my friends, I had to get a haircut. The problem was that you never knew how long it was going to take. You didn't make appointments in those days, you just walked in and waited your turn. It could be five minutes or it could be an hour. This day the shop was full to its small capacity. As Dad opened the screen door to the shop, I immediately spotted my two cousins and a friend in the waiting area. I was already anticipating a fun time when my dad, seeing a full shop, yanked me out of the doorway and back onto the sidewalk. Without saying a word we were in the car heading home. He was not one for waiting. I guess he didn't want to miss an episode of the "Life and Times of Wyatt Earp".

As the years went by I always got my haircuts at Joe's. Joe passed away many years ago and the shop is now run by his family. The noise level is considerably lower now, and the clientele has changed dramatically. The hair that's cut from my head is now gray, and there is less of it. Whenever I go in that barbershop, my mind goes back to the days when Joe and his buddies would argue about everything from taxes to baseball. I guess time changes everything.

Note: Santa Claus paid us a visit at our elementary school one year. In that red Santa's suit and under that white beard (as we all knew), it was "Joe the Barber".

8 MY GANG

Most of us can remember our first friends. In many cases they lived very close to us. These friends were our neighbors and, in many instances, our relatives. My first friends were Marylou Garganigo, Dominic DiBenedetto, Nello Coppellotti, Guy Ferrante, Pauly Bianchi, and my cousins Jack and Bob Zona. Other than the adults in my life, these kids were the closest to me.

Marylou was the little, very blonde girl who lived across from Spag's parking lot. We did everything together. Wherever she'd go, I would follow. It even got to the point that in first grade when our class was being led to the boys and girls bathrooms, I was following her right into the girls' room. All of a sudden I felt Mrs. Hebert, our first grade teacher, yank me out of line and put me in the boy's line. I just thought if she was going there, I must have to go there too.

Dominic, or Donnie, as we called him, lived on Dewey Road, not too far from my house on Baker Ave. Donnie and I played Little League together and, as I mentioned earlier, we even repeated fourth grade together. Donnie's father was a native of Italy. He even spoke to his dog in Italian and the dog understood! Going to Donnie's house was a real treat. You see, his family lived in the cellar, and I could never understand that.

Nello, on the other hand, came from Italy at the age of seven. Because he spoke no English, he was put back two grades. That's what schools did back then. There were no ESL classes in those days. You would either learn English on your own or risk repeating the grade.

My grandfather would constantly speak to Nello in Italian, but Nello would just smile and answer him in English. Back then, if a person spoke in a foreign language, English, usually accented, was learned as quickly as possible. It had its good points and bad. Guy lived on Route 9 across from St. Anne's Church. His family and mine went back two generations. Along with Marylou, Donnie, and Nello, Guy was in first grade with us. Whenever there was a ballgame in the neighborhood, Guy was there. In our pickup baseball games, he was always the third baseman. That's because his favorite player was Eddie Matthews of the Milwaukee Braves.

Pauly, or Pauly B, was a year younger than we were, but hung with us from the beginning. He was there at any birthday party or sports function. Once again, Pauly's family and mine went back generations.

This brings me to probably the closest two kids to me from the old neighborhood. Not only were they my friends, but they happen to be my cousins. Jack and Bob's father was my mother's brother. Our two families were very close. Many times we vacationed together. As families, the three of us went to church together, played Little League together, and even went to Boston Red Sox games together. Although they didn't live as close to me as the others, we were still together almost all the time.

Time has aged us all. As of this writing, we're all in our mid-sixties and on Medicare. Sadly, Jack and Bob passed away way too soon. Jack succumbed to a massive heart attack at age 49 and Bob died of cancer at 60. I often wonder what it would be like if they were still around. I have no doubt we'd still be close. But I speak to them often in my mind.

9 DR. FOSSNER

Not too long ago, I had an 8 a.m. appointment at the doctor's office. I drove up to this huge medical office building, took the elevator up to the third floor, checked in, and waited for about an hour. As I was ready to walk out, my name was finally called. I entered a small examining room and waited some more. By the time I left the building, it must have been two hours later. This is a far cry from a doctor's office visit back in the '50s and early '60s.

Our family doctor was a short, bespectacled, white-haired man by the name of Dr. Mervin Fossner. As a young boy, I had bouts with all the childhood illnesses, such as chicken pox, mumps, and measles. Dr. Fossner would pull up to our house in his big black Buick and, immediately, I knew everything was going to be fine. I can still see him in his long black overcoat, his doctor's bag hanging from one arm, taking short quick steps up the cement sidewalk to the side door of our house.

Dr. Fossner would always great my grandfather first. His voice was deep and clear with no accent. He would say, "Hi Vito," to which my grandfather would replay, "Hi dottor." That's doctor, half English and half Italian.

Dr. Fossner would then turn to me and ask, "What's wrong with you today?" With that, he would take out of his black medical bag a silver little disc attached to two small plastic hoses. That was his stethoscope. As he placed it on my chest it was so cold it felt like an icicle. After a few minutes of checking various areas of my upper body,

Dr. Fossner would fish through his bag and come out with my remedy. After the doctor had a couple of quick glasses of wine with my grandfather, Dad would gladly pay the 5dollar fee for the doctor's visit. Dr. Fossner would jump into his Buick and speed off to his next house call.

As the years went on, Dr. Fossner stopped making house calls unless it was an emergency. We then had to drive to his big stucco house on Pleasant Street in Worcester. His office and examining room were on the first floor, while he and his wife lived on the second floor. Mrs. Fossner would always find time to come down to say hello to my parents. Remember, because my mother couldn't drive, both parents usually came with me.

In the past few years, for whatever reason, I've had the occasion to pass by Dr. Fossner's old office. The house still looks basically the same, but I think it's been divided into three apartments. The old driveway is still there and, if I look really hard, I can see Dr. Fossner's big black Buick parked alongside the house.

There are no more Dr. Fossners. We do have large medical buildings and long waits to be seen. I think of Dr. Fossner now and then, and still wonder what he had in that little black bag that always made me feel better.

Bob, Cousin Frank, and me in 1958.

I'm in front of my grandfather's chicken coop 1954.

Christmas Day Party with Dad and Cousins Bob and Jack Zona.

Dad and I at my first communion 1957

Mom and Dad Boston Common 1945

Mrs. Phillips 2nd Grade
I'm in the middle row, fourth from the left,
Donnie and Nello middle row far right.

Ms. Clark's 3rd grade class.
Marylou, front row far left, Guy Ferrante top row middle

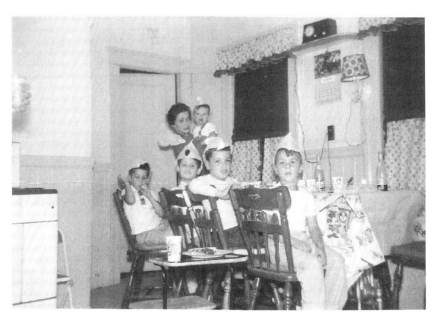

My birthday party with Bob and Jack Zona, cousins Frankie Viscardi,
and Judy Viscardi holding Gerry Viscardi.
Picture taken at Baker Ave 1957

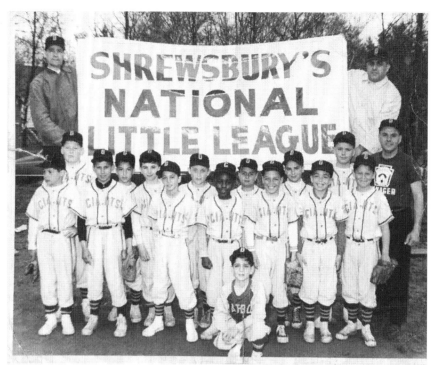

My little league team the 1960 Giants

Official family portrait taken at Baker Ave house 1957.
Notice old washing machine with rollers on the left.

Shrewsbury street 1961 after our little league game.
That's my mother holding my brother in the middle.
Notice the prices

10 DAD's NEW '55 FORD

Back in the mid '50s when a family bought a new car, it was a big event. This was the case when my dad brought home our brand new, shiny 1955 Ford Fairlane. The car was deep green with a wrap-around front window. All the neighbors came over to look at it and kick the tires. It had very little chrome for its day and it wasn't automatic. Furthermore, it wasn't a Cadillac, Buick or even a Pontiac. It was a Ford! Plain and simple. One of our neighbors had a Cadillac. Another had a Buick. We had a stinkin' Ford. When I asked my dad, "Why didn't you buy a Buick?" He said, "Only rich people can afford those cars. A Buick? That's almost a Cadillac."

Cars in those days were almost always owned and driven by men. My dad would always refer to his car as "she." He might say *she's running a little rough* or *she's peppy*. This meant the car had good pickup.

What I never understood was, as soon as the new car arrived in our driveway, he'd say, "Let's take her for a ride and see how she handles the bumps." The roughest, bumpiest roads were a good test for that new Ford. Dad would always end the ride by saying, "She handles the bumps pretty well."

Sundays were always our family ride day. The big decision was always asked by my father to my mother, "Where do you wanna go?" It could be the Clinton Dam, Worcester Airport, Wachusett Mountain, or Meola's Ice Cream Store. This Sunday would be a little different ride.

Dad suggested we take a ride by Bob Cousy's house. After all, he did live on

Chamberlain Parkway in Worcester. Wasn't that ironic! The street where Bob Cousy lived had the name of the Boston Celtics' most hated rival, Wilt "The Stilt" Chamberlain. I didn't care, I just wanted to see his house.

You see, back then Bob Cousy was the Larry Bird, Michael Jordan, or Lebron James of his time. He was, by many accounts, the greatest basketball player in the world. This was a chance to see his house. Today's athletes live in gated communities or so far away from the public you never see them or their homes.

There we were, my dad with his wide brimmed Stetson hat and half chewed cigar, my mother with her kerchief wrapped around the top of her jet back hair, my aunt with her gray hair blowing in the wind, and my baby brother jumping in between the front and back seats. There were no seat belts or car seats. I was the only normal one of that bunch.

We turned slowly from Pleasant Street to Chamberlain Parkway, which was a slight incline. It seemed like it took forever to get up that street. But just then my dad pointed out the window and said, "There's Cousy's house." Wait, as we approached, there was a car pulling into Cousy's driveway. Could it possibly be him? Could I really get to see him? In a flash a thought struck me. *What if Bob Cousy, the greatest basketball player in the world, would see me with these weird people? What would he think of me? I can't let this happen. I know what I'll do. I'll duck down behind the front seat.* This is exactly what I did. As I looked up from my crouched down position, I saw my father raise his big right hand and yell, "Hi Bob!"

In the course of our lives, we all have certain regrets. Even as an 11-year-old, I immediately found this out. I missed the only chance I would ever have to say hi to the greatest basketball player in the world. I'd eventually have a chance to meet him again, which I will describe later in this book, but thanks to our
1955 Ford, I at least got to see his house.

Many years have passed since that Sunday afternoon. I often wonder whatever happened to that '55 Ford. I sure would love to have it back. But more importantly, I'd love to have Dad back.

11 SCHOOL ATTIRE

I am truly amazed at the way kids dress to go to school these days. Shorts, tank tops, and flip flops seem to be the order of the day. I was walking into this particular high school one morning and in front of me was a guy dressed in a sweatshirt, jeans, and sneakers, and carrying a book bag strapped to his shoulders. He was a teacher!

Dressing for school in the 1950's was completely different than now. My mother always made sure I was dressed perfectly. My button-up shirt was without one wrinkle, my pants were perfectly cuffed, and my socks would match my pants. The shoes had to be polished and shiny. Most of the boys were dressed similar to each other. The girls, on the other hand, were held to a higher standard. They wore pleated skirts with a button-up blouse, white ankle socks, and shoes with a strap crossing over their instep. (mary-janes).

I usually kept my hair short. In those days we called that hairstyle a butch or a crew cut. The girl's sported ponytails, pigtails or neck length hair. I think sometimes our mothers were in competition with each other to see who could dress their kid the best.

This is just the way it was back then. Again, the way students dressed in 1958 was very different than today. I've even seen some boys come to school with wrinkled shirts. Imagine that...

This doesn't have anything to do with school dress, but I thought I'd bring it up anyway. The subject is food in the classroom. In elementary school, we were allowed a 15-minute break in the morning. This was called recess. Our mothers gave us *recess cookies*. Other than lunch, this was the only time we could have food in school. One time, while I was rushing out of the house, my mother yelled, "You forgot your recess." This is what sustained us until lunch.

While substitute teaching at another particular school, I'd even see students coming into first period eating cereal and fruit in a cup. Things sure have changed.

12 NORTH SHORE SCHOOL

Elementary schools were decidedly different in the 1950s. Just about all the principals were men. As a student, you'd never see a principal. They wouldn't even say a kind word to you. These principals were there for one thing and one thing only: discipline! To be sent to the principal's office meant you were afraid for you physical well-being.

Harry J. was our principal. He ruled North Shore School with an iron fist. He would've made a great dictator. In my seven years there, I don't think I ever saw Harry J. smile.

Harry J. stood about 5'6" tall, slightly built, and bald. He managed to drag about sixteen hairs across the top of his head. Today we call it a comb-over. Harry J. would occasionally, randomly walk into a classroom and observe for about five minutes. Whenever that happened, the whole class would be afraid to move or speak. Cornball, as we called the Principal, would periodically adjust his pants by putting one hand in front of his belt buckle and the other in the small of his back. With that, he would pull both up at once. It was kind of comical.

Lunchtime was Harry J. at his best. If, in his mind, the lunchroom was too loud, he would stop us from talking altogether. Should any students speak, they would lose their playground privilege. There was one incident in particular that involved my friend Ralph and me. As we were waiting in the lunch line, Ralph felt he should be closer in line to the food servers. This meant cutting ahead of me! I knew that wasn't going to happen! As he tried to pass me, I quickly put my left arm up and braced it against the cement block wall entrance to the kitchen. Ralph pushed and I pushed back, back and forth until we both felt a strong hand grab our shirt collars. It was Harry J. He proceeded to shake us violently. When he finally finished we were taken out of lunch line and told to sit on the stage steps without lunch or playground time. Try doing that to a student today!

The kitchen cooks were Mary Driscoll and Hilda Anish. They were our mothers away from home. Whenever we'd bring our lunch trays to the cleaning area, Hilda would always make us eat our green beans. They watched over us like hawks. Oh, by the way, lunches were 25 cents and milk was 2 cents!

Today, North Shore School no longer exists. In the mid-1970s, one wing burned and was never replaced. A preschool addition was added where our playground once was, and the cafeteria/gym is now a local TV studio. It is now called Parker Road Preschool. I often wonder if the kids today realize how nice their principals are and how approachable they can be.

Another aspect of today's schools is parent pickup. At the end of every school day there are about 25-30 parents waiting to give their children a ride home. I know, because every Tuesday I'm one of them. My daughter is working so I have to pick up my granddaughter, Rachel. Why she can't ride the bus is beyond me. In 1960, at North Shore School, there was no such thing as parent pickup. Some of us rode the Worcester buses home and some of us walked. I was a walker. How could we have parent pickup? Our families only had one car, and even if we did have two cars most of our mothers couldn't drive anyway. So, as I'm waiting in the parent pickup line these days, I always think about North Shore School without parent pickup. Times certainly do change.

13 MRS. COLLINS' 4TH GRADE

One of the most traumatic events in the early life of a grade school student is to be forced to repeat a grade. To not move on with the rest of your class is a severe jolt to a child's confidence and self-worth. The further one progresses in elementary school, the rougher this is for a child to accept. This is what happened to me as a nine-year-old 4th grader.

Mrs. Collins was, by our standards, an elderly teacher by the time we had her in 4th grade. To illustrate this even further, she had my mother as a student many years before. She probably started teaching in the late 1920s, so by the 1960s, time had passed her by. At the time that she became our teacher she was, I'd say, in her mid-60s, but looked much older.

Her style of dress closely resembled the teacher in the movie, "A Christmas Story." Female teachers, in those days, very seldom colored their hair. Mrs. Collins was no different. To see her in her classroom was surely a throwback to the 1940s.

She wore her gray hair up and at the top of her head was a tightly constructed bun. She dressed in a printed smock that extended down below her knees. At the top of her smock, where the top button was, she had a gold brooch attached to the button. At a quick glance she bore an amazing resemblance to the portrait of George Washington on the dollar bill.

Mrs. Collins ran her classroom like a Catholic Sunday School. Framing the chalkboard, and around the room, were colored drawings depicting various religious saints and saviors. That wouldn't go over very well today. Remember, this was a public school.

Mrs. Collins' voice came out in a very low monotone, which made for some very boring classes. If you were caught either not paying attention, which was very difficult, or causing a disruption, she had a great way to embarrass you.

For whatever reason, on this one occasion I wasn't paying attention. Mrs. Collins came over to me and while tapping me on the head, said, "Pay attention young man." When she would say this, it would be followed by a long pause that would draw everyone's attention, and then she would say, "Now, for the people who want to learn."

The Iowa Standardized Test was a good way to measure intelligence. It's probably comparable to the MCAS test of today. A perfect score on the Iowa Test was 100. As Mrs. Collins gave instructions, I decided something else on my mind was more important. Being afraid to ask her to repeat the directions, I did something to really embarrass myself. I filled in the circles at random without even reading the question. Out of a possible 100, my score was 18. Imagine that! Eighteen!

When our test scores came home, my mother was enraged! She immediately showed my father and his reply was, "The guy's dumb." To make matters worse, Mrs. Collins sat us in class according to our test results. What a situation that was.

My cousin, Jack, was also in our class. Jack was one of those kids who could read a newspaper in 10 minutes, finish a book in a day and calculate major league batting averages in seconds. He finished with an almost perfect score. Mrs. Collins seated us according to our test scores. That meant Jack was first in the class and I was last. What an embarrassment!

One of Mrs. Collins' favorite learning tools was a spelling bee, and I really excelled at spelling. But even at my best, I couldn't beat Jack. We would usually have our spelling bee on a Friday. Whoever won the contest was awarded a brand new shiny quarter by Mrs. Collins.

Guess who always seemed to win that quarter... My cousin Jack. As well as I could spell, I could never unseat him as champion of the spelling bee, except for this one particular Friday afternoon.

The bee was moving along just as I figured, with my cousin firmly in control and poised to win. Then, like a miracle, it happened! He messed up on a lesser word. I couldn't believe it; my cousin Jack, smartest kid in class and maybe the school, actually misspelled a word. My heart started racing. I can win this! The rest of these kids can't spell with me. I'm finally going to get that shiny new quarter.

Just as I'm set to win, the unthinkable happened. The bell rang for dismissal! This was just my stinkin' rotten luck. Mrs. Collins assured us, the remaining contestants, that we'd finish this on Monday. It never happened and I never did get that quarter, but to this day, I know I would have won that spelling bee.

The worst rejection a fourth grader can possibly have is to be made to repeat a grade or, as we called it, to stay back. This is exactly what happened to me that awful year. I'm not saying I didn't deserve it, because I did, but it still hurts to see all your friends move to the next grade and you're stuck in a room with what I considered, third graders.

Three of us were kept back that fateful June of 1959. Yes, Butchie, Donnie, and I had to repeat the fourth grade. Mrs. Collins even called me up to her desk the next day to last day of school and in her monotone voice said, "Look at this, young man." As I looked down at her wrinkled hand holding my report card, she pointed to one line, it said, "This pupil will report in September to grade four." That was it! I was done! At that point the world could've ended and I wouldn't have cared one bit. What an awful and embarrassing summer this would be.

If that should happen to a student today there would be a meeting of everyone involved in his or her education. Unfortunately, not one of our mothers ever called or questioned t h a t t e a c h e r ' s d e c i s i o n. That's j u s t t h e w a y i t w a s b a c k t h e n. Teachers were always right.

In retrospect, it probably helped me more later in life. I was, in reality, immature for my age in that first year of fourth grade. In fact, there are times now that my wife will call me immature. Some things never change.

14 I COULDN'T HOLD IT
(THE THIRD BASE INCIDENT)

Every kid, or almost every kid, wanted to play baseball in those days. In our end of town, there was a Farm League for the beginners and Little League for the more proficient kids. To play Little League, with full baseball uniforms, was the goal of every one of us. The problem was that only a very few Farm Leaguers made it.

When I turned eight my dad decided, after playing ball in the yard, it was time to see just how well I could play. He signed me up to play Farm League baseball. Dad also coached my team. We were called The Cardinals. There were no uniforms, but we did have black hats with a big red 'C' on them. It was great! Dad brought the team's equipment home and I used it. I was the hit of the neighborhood.

Our games were played at Coolidge School Field. My dad put me at shortstop, not realizing that I wasn't very good at fielding — but boy, could I hit! In this one particular game, after a pretty good hit, I ended up on third base and feeling pretty good about myself. It was then my nightmare started. I had to go to the bathroom!

What should I do? I was on third base. A simple hit and I'd reach home and, more importantly, get to relieve myself. I could call timeout and maybe get someone to run for me, but then, the manager, my dad, would want to know why. I didn't know what to do. All I knew was I had to go immediately, if not sooner!

As I stood on the base, the unthinkable happened. I had no choice but to let it go and satisfy my kidneys. I could feel "the liquid" trickling down my left leg. I was afraid to look down. I finally did, and didn't like the result. The liquid was streaming slowly onto the white base and spilling into the soft sand around it. I did eventually score and ran quickly to the bench. I strategically went to the far end of the bench and sat on the ground, wet pants and all. I could hide there. I don't think at that point, anyone realized what happened. But I did!

However, I needed a quick excuse not to go back on the field. I could say I didn't feel well or I was tired, but Dad wouldn't buy either of those lame excuses. While I was cowering at the end of the bench, another stroke of bad luck hit me. Our team batted around and it was my turn to hit again! Now what do I do? Do I not say anything and maybe no one will notice, or do I tell my father and hope he'll understand? I chose the latter and boy, was it the wrong choice. The moment of truth was now here. As Dad came over to my spot on the ground, he reminded me to get on deck, which meant I was the next batter. When I didn't make a move he asked me again. "Are you gonna hit?" I sheepishly looked up and said, "I can't." His reply was, "Why not?" I pointed out with my eight-year-old index finger to the wetness down the side of my left leg.

I thought by showing him my problem he'd understand and say, without fanfare, "OK, you can sit out." Again I was wrong. He looked down at me and said, "Are you gonna get up or not?" With that I shook my head and said, "I can't," for the second time. At that point he said, loud enough for the whole team to hear, "OK you, get outta here." Where was I going to go? So I asked him, "Where do you want me to go?" "I don't care where you go, just get outta here!" he replied. I picked up my glove and, as the rest of the team watched, slowly walked to our car. A long walk for an embarrassed eight year old.

The car seemed to be five miles away, but in reality it was only about 200 feet. As I slowly opened the car door, I tossed my glove in first, then got in and immediately slouched down in the front seat. The game seemed to never end. Some kids came riding by the car and tried to peek in at me. I could hear snickering. It was absolutely awful. The ride home wasn't any better. Dad didn't speak to me at all. I'll never forget that day. It's probably the most embarrassed I've ever been. And do you think Dad ever apologized to me for that incident? No way!

After that experience, whenever or wherever I played, whether it was high school, college, or semi-pro baseball, I always went to the bathroom before the game!

15 SLEEPING OUT

At the beginning of the '60s we were in our pre-teen years and always looking for something to do. "Sleeping out" was always fun. A night out under the stars was a very liberating experience. No mom and dad to tell us what to do, what to eat, or what to wear.

To sleep out you needed a sleeping bag, plenty of bug spray, and no fear of the dark. More importantly, you needed permission from your parents. That could be a tough sell. After a little begging and pleading they would usually give in. Of course, my mother would want to know the names of the kids I'd be sleeping out with. I'd quickly throw out the names Charlie Besardi, Pauly Bianchi, Donnie DiBenedetto, Mikey D'Errico, and Jimmy Campbell. Then I would add, "We're sleeping out in Mikey's back yard." That sealed it. My mother liked Mikey's mother, which meant it was ok. Little did she know what was on our minds.

We got into our sleeping bags around 10 p.m. and after a few hours of talking and semi-sleep, we were ready to start our journey. We were about to find out what Shrewsbury looks like in the wee small hours of the morning. We shed our sleeping bags and started down Dewey Road toward Boston Turnpike.

Back then the stores were closed by 10:00 pm. There was nothing open 24 hours. Remember, this was 1962. Any place open all night was still twenty years away or on the Massachusetts Turnpike. The stores were dimly lit with night lights, and the traffic lights still went from red to yellow to green, but there were no cars to obey them. It was a very weird sight.

We all wondered what It would be like to swim in our local swimming hole, Jordan Pond, at two o'clock in the morning. That's what we should do. We all agreed. As we walked down Plainfield Ave, a cat crying or a dog barking might break the night silence. At the end of the street was the path we would have to take to get to the pond. The trouble was that it was a winding path with tree branches sticking out along the way. To get hit with one of those branches, a person could lose an eye. We had to be very careful.

With only the light coming from a full moon we made our way toward the beach. It was at this time Charlie decided to set off an M-80 firecracker in the air over the pond. The sound was deafening. It really broke the night silence. I thought for sure the police would be called.

As we got closer to the beach, I could see the sand on the shore of the pond being illuminated from the unusually bright moonlight. We could hear moaning and groaning coming from the darkened picnic area. It became very clear to us that it was a man and a woman obviously enjoying each other. The decision was quickly made not to swim there.

Plan B was to trek down to Lake Quinsigamond to another friend's house that had a rope swing that went over the water. Once there we stripped off our clothes and made like Tarzan minus the loincloth.

Our friend with the rope swing passed away some years ago and condominiums now dominate the shoreline.

Charlie, Pauly, Donnie, Mikey, Jimmy and I are all in our mid-60s now. We still get together a couple times a month and talk about that night back in August 1962. To this day, even though our parents are gone, I don't think they ever knew what we did when we slept out that night.

Or did they…

16 I'M A LITTLE LEAGUER

In 1959, just about every kid in Farm League aspired to play Little League baseball. Why not? In Farm League we played in our regular clothes and on fields that had more weeds than grass. At times you couldn't tell where the infield ended and the outfield began. By contrast, if you were one of the chosen few to be selected to play Little League, you reached the 'Promised Land'. The next step, we thought, was the Boston Red Sox.

Tryouts for Little League were particularly stressful for all of us back then. As I remember, it was always cold and windy on tryout day. The Little League managers and coaches pinned a white sheet of paper on our backs with hand-written black numbers on them. I guess it was easier to tell us apart that way. At times, a certain manager might ask our name. That was, to us, always a good sign. It usually took about two days for the managers to decide who they wanted, then the waiting game began. For the next week I stayed close to the phone, although at nine years old I didn't think I'd be picked. If I were 10 or 11, I'd have a better chance of making Little League. After all, my dad was still managing my Farm League team, the Cardinals. I'd be a star on that team. Dad explained I'd have one more year of experience playing organized baseball and at 10, I'd definitely be ready for Little League.

It was Saturday morning, a week after tryouts and I hadn't received a call, when a thought went through my mind. What if I did get picked? What should I do? Refuse, and stay in Farm League or move up to Little League? I guess I'll cross that bridge when I get to it. But it certainly would be great to wear a full baseball uniform and play on a grass field with actual base paths.

As I sat at our kitchen table reading the Worcester Telegram about the Boston Red Sox —Ted Williams was coming back for the 1960 season — our yellow wall phone rang. I picked up the receiver fully expecting the call to be one of my mother's girlfriends, but low and behold the voice on the other end was that of a man. He immediately identified himself as the manager of the Giants in the Shrewsbury National Little League. I was selected by him to be a member of that team. Any thoughts of remaining in Farm League were quickly dashed from my mind. Without hesitation, I accepted his offer to be a member of the Giants.

You see, as a nine-year-old in Little League with 10-, 11-, and 12-year-olds being the better players, my playing time would be minimal at best. There was no two inning rule in those days, which required every kid to play at least two innings per game. One could literally sit on the bench all season and not play one inning. This was something to consider. In Farm League, with my dad managing, I'd play most likely every inning of every game. My father even suggested I stay in Farm League for that reason. To me, it was a simple decision, I was now a Giant.

Dad was right. I played very little that year and to tell you the truth, I didn't want it any other way. I was literally out of my league. I couldn't compete with those older kids and I knew it, but at least I got to wear the uniform.

At the end of the last game the manager sat the whole team down and asked, "Did everybody pass this year?" This meant, did we all move up a grade in school. I sat at the end of the bench and didn't say a word. How could I! That would be the ultimate embarrassment. Many years later I happened to run into my former manager. I told him how I didn't own up to the fact that I actually did stay back and never admitted it that day he asked our team. He told me not to
worry about it and that it was a long time ago. I didn't find out until I read his obituary that my manager was a tail gunner on a B29 Bomber over Germany during World War II. I thought that staying back in school was nothing compared to what he went through.

My third year on the Giants brought about another incident. I am now eleven years old and one of the premier players on the team, if not the league. The all-star team, which was comprised of the best players in the league, was about to be selected. Now, picking the team was usually done at a neutral location. The fire station was always as good as a place as any to select the team.

Unfortunately, one of the fathers insisted the voting be done at his house where there would be a wide variety of food. A few of the managers wanted to keep it at the fire station, but the majority won out. This particular father had one thing on his mind and that was to get his son, who didn't deserve it, on that all-star team.

The move paid off. Not only did his son make the all-star team, he beat out my best friend who, at the time, was leading the league in homers. How do you think I felt when my dad came home and told me the bad news? I had the unenviable job of telling my best friend the reason he didn't make the team. He was so disappointed he never played baseball again. To this day, whenever I see him, we always bring this up.

As I mentioned in my introduction, race kept a low profile in the early '60s in Shrewsbury. It was never spoken of or brought up. The only two African American kids in our league were on our team. In fact, their father would fill in as our manager when my dad worked late at his factory. But there was always that undercurrent depicting African Americans as not like the rest of us. To us, as eleven and twelve year olds, they were just people.

This one particular game, I was pitching into the fourth inning and getting hit pretty well. My dad, the manager, had to work late which meant managerial duties fell to Mr. Truesdale who was African-American. Now normally if my father was managing, I'd be taken immediately out of the game. This time, Mr. Truesdale motioned to the umpire to call timeout and he calmly walked to the pitcher's mound where I was stomping around. Figuring I'd be taken out, I got ready to flip the baseball to him. Not only did he not take me out, but he proceeded to let me know he was sticking with me because he had confidence in me. That's all I needed to know. I ended up winning that game, and I'll never forget the confidence Mr. Truesdale showed in me. It made all the difference in my mind.

The next day when I told my dad about the game, I mentioned Mr.

Truesdale's talk with me at the mound. He said he liked Mr. Truesdale and that he was a good man. This directly contradicted some of the negative comments I heard him make about African Americans. At this point, as an 11-year-old, I'm confused. Now, as we're driving home from our Little League game, I said to my father, "I thought you said you didn't like colored people." My dad didn't answer and kept on driving. After about 15 or 20 seconds, which seemed much longer, he responded with an answer that confused me even more. "He's different," Dad said about Mr. Truesdale. It was later in life that I finally figured out what my father was trying to say. The world was a lot different back then, or was it?

17 THE DENTIST

We all have certain things in our lives that we fear. It could be flying; being in small closed-in areas; the dark; or even going to the dentist. At the tender age of 11, going to the dentist was by far my biggest fear. If I knew I had a dentist appointment coming up, it would be impossible for me to sleep the night before. Almost every time an appointment was due, my father, who always took me, knew he was going to have a fight on his hands.

As I remember, it was on a day in May 1961, in the middle of Little League baseball season, when it just so happened I had an appointment with the dentist. The whole day in school all I could think about was sitting in that dentist chair and getting drilled. This wasn't just a cleaning, this was going to be genuine torture. Even worse than the drilling was that long, scary Novocain needle. It always felt like that needle would come out the other side of my cheek and all I knew was that I had to do something about the situation!

My father was due home from his job at the factory around 3:30 pm. I thought, *Maybe he'll forget about the appointment. I'm not even going to mention it. We can always go some other time. That's it! I'll act like it's just another day. Being a coach on our team, he's probably thinking more about me pitching tonight than anything else.* That was my first mistake.

I was in the kitchen doing my homework when I heard my dad's car pull into the garage. The moment of truth was quickly approaching. I said I was doing my homework, but really nothing could've been farther from the truth. As he came through the door from the garage and into the kitchen, he turned to me and

said, "Are you ready? Let's go." My worst fears were confirmed. He didn't forget at all. In fact, I think he was looking forward to it.

I had to do something and it had to be quick. With that, I jumped up from the table, let out a resounding "NO" and proceeded to lock myself in my bedroom. Now, if this had been our old house on Baker Ave, I have no doubt he would have kicked the door open. But because this was our brand new house, Dad had to resort to other measures. While he was trying to figure out what to do, I took the opportunity to exit the house into the front yard. I felt I had a better chance outside. A chase ensued. As he ran after me, around the tall maple tree in our front yard, I knew it was useless. I figured I was safer behind a locked door. What did I do? I locked myself in the same room again. Now my father had a dilemma: how to get me out of that room and to the dentist without causing any damage to the house. He had to think of something.

As I sat in my locked bedroom, I figured Dad would call the dentist and schedule a new appointment. This would buy me a little more time. He came to the door one more time. He yelled through the door, "Come ahn, let's go!" To which I answered, "No". He then said "Alright, I'll fix you. I'm gonna call the manager and make you quit Little League." That was it. Dad had pulled his trump card. He even had the phone in his hand, ready to make the call to the manager of my team. He really had me and now the ball was in my court. Could he really do this? Could he really make me quit Little League? I couldn't take that chance. I finally did go to the dentist and I guess, looking back now, I'm glad I did, but I did so reluctantly.

Many years later, I was in Dad's hospital room after his heart surgery. I had to ask him the question that was bothering me for many years. I asked him, "Dad, remember back when I wouldn't go to the dentist? Would you really have made me quit Little League?

Would you really have called the manager?" Dad looked at me, smiled and said, "I don't think so." Four days later, Dad died of complications from heart surgery. At least I got my answer.

There's not a day that I don't think about him. I now know why he did the things he did. I never knew how much my dad loved me until I had my own children. I guess it's true: everything comes full circle and, thanks to my dad, I still have my teeth!

18 SHREWSBURY STREET

In the Worcester of the 1950s, it seemed as though every ethnic group had its own section. The Polish lived in and around Millbury Street, The Irish in Main South, the French had the area around Cambridge Street, and the Swedes claimed two neighborhoods: Quinsigamond Village and Greendale. The East Side, once settled by the Irish, was now almost all Italian. Shrewsbury Street was the hub of activity for these Italian Americans.

Back in those days, Shrewsbury Street had three generations of Italian Americans. First, you had the immigrants, who were "right off the boat." Then there was their offspring, or the first-generation Italian Americans. Lastly, the second-generation included kids my age. These three groups constituted Shrewsbury Street in the '50s and early '60s.

The United States Almanac listed Italians as the largest foreign-born group living in the USA as of 1960. From 1880 to 1921, the era of the great migration, over four million people left Italy, mostly from Southern Italy, for the US. "Little Italys" sprang up in most major cities in the East. Worcester, with its Shrewsbury Street on the East Side, was no different.

If one was to describe Shrewsbury Street in those days, it would be necessary to include the numerous mom and pop grocery stores, social clubs, bookie joints, and of course, Our Lady of Mount Carmel Church. On any evening, mostly during the summer, you'd see men at various locations along the street playing an Italian game called *mortah*, or just trying to solve the problems of the world.

Three languages were spoken on Shrewsbury Street. Back then you would hear Italian, English, and a mixture of both. Isn't it funny;, all these foreign-born Italians never thought they had an accent!

On Shrewsbury Street, the third weekend in August brought about the three-day "Feast of San Vitaliano." He was the Patron Saint of Sparanise, Italy, which is where my mother's people came from. The three days of the feast included Italian singers, parades and, on Sunday night, a huge fireworks display that always ended with the American flag lit by ground fireworks and accompanied by the National Anthem.

Saturday mornings you could always smell the sweet aroma of fresh-baked Italian bread coming from any one of the several bakeries on the street. Saturdays also brought about another interesting aspect of our culture. It was the illegal numbers game, which is now called the State Lottery. My Dad would ask me, "Hey you, gimme *tree* numbers." After I quickly picked out the first numbers that came into my head, he would write them down on any scrap of paper he could find. We would then dash up to Shrewsbury Street to this little hole-in-the-wall building called the Corner Spa. Now, I'm about seven years old sitting in a double-parked car -- while it's running -- waiting for my dad to play his "lucky numbers." Within about five minutes there must have been 10-15 guys going in and out of the shop. I suggested to Dad that the store does quite a business and he promptly told me to "never mind about what *dey* do in *dat* store." That meant it was none of my business. I never asked again. But can you imagine leaving a seven-year-old in a parked, running car today? That's just the way it was back then.

Another facet of the illegal world my dad was involved in was football games, college and professional, and involved giving points to the lesser team. This made all teams equal.

Dad would get a new crop of cards every Tuesday. By Friday, I'd have my teams picked. All my picks were random, of course. I must have had a lucky streak, because I hit winning cards four out of five weeks in a row. His customers wouldn't make their selections until they took a look at my selections. I had them baffled.

They probably thought I had some secret insight into these games.

Little did they know, I was only guessing. What else would you expect from a nine-year old.

Shrewsbury St is different now. Most of the old timers have died and their adult children have moved to the suburbs. My father did hit the number once for $550.00. $50 went to the bookie.

19 A NEW PRIEST

Religion, back in the late '50s and early '60s, was very important to most of the families in the neighborhood. It seemed like just about everybody we knew was Catholic, and St. Anne's was our church. From social events that our parents attended, or just going to Mass, other than school, the church was the center of many of our activities. One of our favorite hangouts was the church hall. "The Hall" was a building approximately 50 yards behind the church which housed an indoor basketball court. It was also where our religious education (or " CCD") classes were held.

Our pastor was elderly Father Smith. Father Smith had white receding hair and when he wasn't serving Mass, he could be seen walking around in a floor-length black cassock. Smitty, as we affectionately called him, had that Catholic priest's white collar and a sported black three-corner hat with a black tassel on top. Father Smith never said much to us, but even if he did, we couldn't understand him anyway. His associate, or curate, as he was called in those days, was a very handsome French-Canadian named Father Leon Richard.

Father Richard had dark, olive skin and straight, slightly greased jet black hair. All the parish women loved him and, as I think back, I can see why. He acted as many of the priests did back then. He was generally quiet, reserved and spoke very little to us. There was one time when we were playing basketball in The Hall, Father Richard had to walk across the court. When we stopped the game to let him pass, he called for the basketball. Father Richard calmly took two or three shots at the basket. I think he sank one of the three. That was Father

Richard. The priests in those days pretty much kept their distance from us, but as we shall soon see, that would all change.

We gathered to play basketball in The Hall one particular day when some guy in street clothes came in, looked around and walked quickly over to us as we were picking teams. He glanced down at our feet and as he fixated on mine asked, "What size sneakers do you have?" Surprised and a little bit stunned I said, "Nine." His reply was, "Just my size. Can I borrow them?" Having never had this happen before, I replied, "Sure." This strange guy that none of us knew took my place on our team in our pickup game. Then like a lightning bolt struck me, I said to myself "This must be Father Gonyor! This is the priest who knows the great Bob Cousy"! Father Gonyor would later prove to us that he did indeed know 'The Cooze'.

That day cemented forever my friendship with Father Gonyor. He not only played basketball with us, Father came with our CYC group to Hampton Beach and also took us altar boys to the circus whenever it was in town. He was more of a friend to us than a priest. Catholic Youth Council (CYC) was popular with the young people in those days. CYC sponsored dances, trips to Hampton Beach and ski trips, and we even had our own basketball team. But the biggest CYC event of the year was the annual banquet. This was the night different types of awards were presented to deserving members. Before the awards ceremony, the CYC president usually gave a speech. But one particular night, it would be cut short.

Pat Bourque was president of our CYC. He would later go on to have the distinction of being the only baseball player from Shrewsbury, via St. John's High School, to make it all the way to Major League Baseball. But this night wasn't about baseball.

As I was sitting near the front of The Hall I could hear a low murmur coming from the back. All of a sudden, my row and the rest of the people in The Hall, stood up in unison. What was this commotion? Who could be entering The Hall that would create such a reaction? As I strained my 12-year-old neck to find out, I caught a glimpse of the sight I'd never forget.

Walking directly behind Father Gonyor was the greatest basketball player in the world. Yes, it really was Bob Cousy! The Bob Cousy I watched on TV! The Bob Cousy who won five NBA Championships! This was too good to be true! I'm in the same building as Bob Cousy!

Father Gonyor was true to his word, he really did know The Cooz. What really struck me was the height of Cousy. For years we watched him on a 15-inch black and white TV, and to see him now in person, so tall and tanned, was almost looking like a God coming down the aisle.

He was very gracious to everyone. I think he stayed for hours signing autographs. Years later, while I was teaching a photography course in summer school, I had the pleasure of meeting his daughter. I told her this story.

"The Cooz" is in his eighties now and, unfortunately, just lost his wife. Father Gonyor passed away a few years ago. But that great night will live in my mind forever. I can still see the great Bob Cousy coming down the aisle.

One of our trips to VT in our 55 Ford

Donnie and I in the middle row, Bobby Zona is sitting 2nd from the right and Jack Zona standing back row 4th from the left.

Uncle Ralph's Ford Victoria
That's Spags in the background 1954

Vermont Vacation in the 1951 Plymouth

Widening RT 9 and Harrington approx. 1956

With Bob, Jack & Joel my baby brother, notice my attitude

With Mom in this picture, could my head be any bigger?

With Mom, Uncle John and Vic Zona 1955

With my Grandfather Vito Circa 1954

In front of Uncle Vic's 1954 Ford

20 GOING TO FENWAY

In the course of our lives I believe we all have fantasies. Some people fantasize that they're millionaires, other may fantasize about being a movie star. Still others will fantasize that they are the President. There are all kinds of fantasies. My fantasies, as an 11-year-old, almost always included the Red Sox and Fenway Park. Whether it was playing there or just going to a Red Sox game, Fenway was my ultimate fantasy.

Going to Fenway Park was always an exciting event. First, my dad would pick a date, usually a Friday night or a Saturday afternoon game. Back then, tickets could be bought the same day as the game. Even a Saturday game would attract a crowd of only 15,000, which is a far cry from today when almost every game is a sellout. Ticket prices back then were very affordable. You have to remember this was before free agency. A reserved grandstand seat cost $2, bleacher seats were 75 cents, and box seats, the best seats in the park, were $3.

With the Massachusetts Turnpike (MassPike) still 10-12 years away at the time, Route 9 brought us right into Boston. My anticipation and excitement grew with every mile that drew us closer to the park. The first indication that we actually were going to Fenway was the Carling Brewery in Natick, Mass. My dad would always say, "We're halfway there."

The next point of interest when going to the game popped up in the town of Newton. It was four complete trees growing out of one stump and my dad would always say, "That tree is in *Ripley's Believe It*

54

or Not." Ripley's Believe It or Not was a little article appearing in magazine publications that highlighted the oddities of life.

Route 9 turned into Brookline Ave, which led to Fenway. At this point I was still pretty calm until I saw the light towers. That sent a wave of excitement through me like no other feeling. At the bottom of those light towers was Ted Williams, Jackie Jensen, Frank Malzone, and the rest of the Red Sox. I'd actually be in the same building as these pro baseball players!

We always parked on a side street about 500 yards from the park. It was in front of the old S.S. Pierce building and there was no parking fee. As we got out of the car, my dad always made sure we had our homemade tuna sandwiches, wrapped in tin foil, which by the third inning would be mushy. He didn't feel we should pay 25 cents for a hot dog when we have food at home.

My dad liked to let me bring friends with us to Fenway. Generally, it was my two cousins Bob and Jack, and friends Nello and Donnie. Nello came to this country from Italy at the age of seven and picked up baseball right away. Donnie, (Dominic) lived a couple of streets down on the other side of Spag's parking lot. We all played on the Giants Little League team and we were all Red Sox fans.

The Sox didn't do very well in those days, but that didn't matter to us. All I knew was that we were going to see professional baseball at Fenway Park. We were going to sit in the park and see all these players in color — and not on a 12-inch black and white Admiral TV set.

So there we were all of us walking that short distance to Fenway Park. My father, with his Cupola hat, long pigeon-toed strides, zipped-up sweater and us five kids trying to keep up. When we did reach the park, in most cases it hadn't opened. My dad always liked to get there early. As we stood there, all of a sudden we would hear the sound of the green rippled garage doors opening to the inside of Fenway Park. The crowd around us was sparse, so we took our time getting in. Once in, we made our way through the corral-like railing that led to the brick-enclosed ticket booth. A man behind the bars would asked my dad, "Whatd'ya need?" My dad would ask, "Whatd'ya have in left field?" The ticket man would slowly peel off six 1-inch by 4-inch tickets and my dad would put twelve dollars in the space under the bars. Dad slowly turned in our direction and deliberately passed a ticket to each of us. He then pulled me aside and said, "You betta hold ona dat ticket". If you drop it dat guy ova dere is liable to step on it and I'll have to fight him for it." I guess it was his way of making sure I didn't lose it. After all, it did cost two dollars!

From there, we made our way to the usher at the turnstile. He took the ticket, ripped it in half, and gave part of it back to me. Now we are officially in Fenway Park. We passed by a few program vendors on our way up the ramp that led to our seats. As we walked up the ramp I'd try to hold my excitement, but it just struck me. It was a 10-year-old's' version of Heaven.

As I got to the top of the ramp, the first image to hit me was the green grass. On TV it was always gray. Even more shocking was the contrast between the Red Sox white uniforms and the beautiful green field. My dad checked with an usher who led us to our seats. I still couldn't take my eyes off the field. You see, back then the park was open during batting practice. Sometimes the players would even come over and talk to us!

With the old three-sided batting cage, many batting practice balls would be hit our way. At this time, there was only about a couple hundred people scattered around the park. In the left field grandstand, there were only about 25 kids around us, all with the same idea, to get a baseball. Then, all of a sudden a batted ball comes arching towards us.

Now my father had his own way of dressing. He would wear a button-up sports shirt with the tails hanging out. The shirt had to have two pockets. One pocket for his cigars, Dutch Masters, and the other for his eye glasses. His size-13 shoes were never tied, the result of protruding bunions on each foot. Anytime he tried to run or jump everything would fly out of his pockets. That's just what happened!

As the ball made its way in our direction, my father jumped up on the folding seat, leaped over the next row, and dove for the errant ball. Did he finally get the souvenir for which all fans fight? No, but the kids in the stands around us got scared out of their wits by this madman trying to catch a ball. What a sight it was. As he leaped over the row of seats, his shirt pockets were quickly emptied of cigars or eyeglasses. Not only that, but one of his untied size 13 shoes went flying 5 rows up. To cap it all off, the ball bounced back onto the field!

As the game reached into the 6th or 7th inning, my friends and I were getting tired and bored. To make matters worse, the Red Sox were losing. I asked Dad, "Do you think we can go home now?" This, I thought, was a very legitimate question. His reply was, "I paid for nine innings, I'm gonna see nine innings." And sure enough, we stayed until the final out was made.

Now, whenever I get the chance or have the money, to go to a Sox game, I always get there early and I always stay until the last out. That's what Dad taught me. I paid for nine innings, I'm gonna see nine innings.

21 WE HAVE TO MOVE

In the mid-'50s, the department store known as Spag's was expanding. One by one, owner Anthony Borgatti bought up all our neighbors' properties. What once was a thriving Italian-American community filled with vegetable gardens, pear trees, and grapevines, with a brook running through the middle, was now becoming an asphalt jungle.

Gone were the Garganigos, the Guerras, the Robios, the Borghesanis, the Vesellas, the Viscardis, the Cialones and the Celluccis. We were almost all alone in the middle of this reconstruction. The neighborhood had lost its luster. It would never be the same again. My mother and grandfather knew it. Now came the harsh reality of what to do about it.

Anthony 'Spag" Borgatti was very generous when it came to giving people a fair price for their property. In our case, he was no different. For our house and land, we got a brand-new, state-of-the-art ranch home with one quarter acre of land. It was an offer my mother couldn't refuse. The problem was that living there felt like we had gone from the city to the country. From busy Baker Ave to country Old Mill Road. I think in those days, we saw one car pass by our house every five minutes.

Our house was situated approximately four hundred feet from, appropriately named, Old Mill Pond. This opened up a whole new world for me. New friends and a new activity: ice skating!

I still kept my old friends, but they were now about a quarter-mile away. In my Old Mill surroundings, new names popped up. Names like Roger, Debbie, and Beverly Nolli, Donnie Govoni, Linda Angelico and Paul Lorusso. Having moved closer to my cousins, they would continue to be an important part of my life.

Hockey was now a sport I wanted to play. I first had to learn how to skate. Once I mastered it, the games would start. Because our house was so close to the pond, my garage became the perfect spot for all my friends' skates, shin guards, and hockey sticks.

The enemy of ice is snow. Snow always fouled up everything. Luckily, our neighbor, Mr. Nolli, would plow a large ice area for us. This spot would be big enough for hockey or just plain skating.

Every year the Nollis would sponsor a skating party, which would usually end with us burning the island. It was a harmless fire that wouldn't go anywhere.

Nowadays, I never see anybody skating on Old Mill Pond. I guess there are too many indoor skating rinks. The kids of today will never know the fun we had on Old Mill Pond, playing hockey, having skating parties, or skating all the way up the brook that feeds the pond. We'd do this at night, with only the ice glare to show us the way.

The island is gone now. Back in the '80s the pond was emptied and dredged. Mr. Nolli passed away a few years ago, but I can still hear my mother assuring me by saying, "If Mr Nolli's plowing the pond, it must be safe."

22 SUNDAYS

Sundays were always my favorite day of the week. Fridays were fine with school being over for the week. Saturdays I also enjoyed, but Sundays were the most fun.

In those days, all my relatives lived within walking distance of our house. Sunday mornings would bring us all together at St. Anne's Church, usually the 9 o'clock Mass. In the meantime my dad, who didn't attend church very often, would start the macaroni sauce simmering in a large metal pan. This was an all morning affair.

While the sauce was simmering, he would throw in cut-up steak, pork chops and shredded pieces of chicken. Along with some garlic and peppers, the whole house was filled with this aroma. Dad would then leave to visit his social club for his game of billiards with all his cronies.

Catholic Mass would end at about 10:00, depending on the length of Father Gonyor's sermon. By the time my aunt and I would leave the church, it was probably close to 10:30. My uncle would be waiting for us with my two cousins in his 1950 Dodge. After a quick trip to Whitey's Spa for a newspaper, usually the *Sporting News*, we'd end up at my house on Old Mill Road. The rest of my uncles would soon follow along with their own children. This made for quite a gathering.

The adults would sit and talk about everything from politics to sports. Once in a while my mother and her sisters-in-law would get into a heated discussion, but

it would quickly end with no hard feelings. My uncles never argued. I've often said, if the world was like them there would be no wars.

At about 11:30 a.m. my dad would arrive home and ready for lunch. He always expected to eat at noon sharp. My aunts and uncles would be deep in conversation, but that didn't matter to my dad.

All he knew was that his stomach said he had to eat at 12:00. As conversations were taking place, Dad proceeded to remove the coffee cups and dishes from the table. This action always drew ire from my mother. My uncles knew this would happen and I think they really got a kick out of it. Besides, my dad would always extend an invitation for them to share lunch with him. They never accepted.

The fun part for me, as a 10-year-old, was to be able to play with my cousins well into the afternoon. You see, back then, all businesses were closed on Sunday, except for the small mom and pop stores. Today, Sunday is just like any other day, with everyone rushing around as if it were a regular weekday. In those years, Sunday was truly a family day.

I sometimes think of those Sundays as I rush around to my grandkids' soccer games. It really was much simpler back then.

23 WHAT SWIMMING POOLS?

In today's world every family, or almost every family, has a swimming pool. Some pools are in ground and some are above ground. Pool supply stores are everywhere. This wasn't the case in my world of the 19'50s and early '60s.

At the time, swimming pools were a luxury that only the rich could afford. As I mentioned in the Introduction, our postage-stamp-sized yards were clogged with vegetable gardens, grapevines, and chicken coops. Even if we could afford a pool, which we couldn't, it was considered a waste of land and space. The thinking was, why b u y a pool when we had Lake Quinsigamond and Jordan Pond? What more could a kid want?

Usually after a hot, dusty morning playing baseball on the Ward Field rock pit, we would decide on any one of a number of spots to go swimming. But usually most of these places were on Lake Quinsig.

One day Maironis Park would be our choice, or Olympia Park, or we'd even get on our bicycles and ride over to Tatassit Beach. Tatassit was the most fun. That beach had a high slide that would shoot you into the oil-slicked lake water. It also had a cable that extended almost the length of the beach. Fifteen feet above the ground was the platform we had to stand on. Once there, we would grab two handles extended from the cable. The handles were attached to a wheel that would carry us down to water's level. It made us feel like Tarzan.

The only problem with Tatassit was it cost money to swim there. There was also Sunset Beach, but that was too far away. Other places we went were Solomon Pond in Northboro, Regatta Point, or Holland Pool on Lincoln Street. To get to these places, our parents would have to take us. Green Hill P a r k was also a good place to swim, as long as you didn't mind the carp swimming around you.

* Carp is a huge garbage-eating fish. It looks something like a blownup goldfish.

There was one family that did have a swimming pool. It w a s a beautiful in-ground pool. We used to look at it from a hill behind their house, hoping we would get an invitation to join them. The drawback was that they had only girls in the family.

They were certainly not going to let a bunch of sweaty boys jump into their pool with their daughters. But there was always hope. Eventually we did get invited in and we had a great time. It was so much more fun to swim without stepping on rocks or weeds. I even asked my father if we could put a pool in our back yard. Dad looked at me and said," What are you, nuts"!

The pool is gone now and the hill where we once stood and gazed at it has a house built on it. Even a few of my friends who jumped in the pool with me that first time, have passed away. But my memories of that sparkling pool are forever etched in my mind.

24 FINALLY A LITTLE BROTHER

Families in the '50s averaged three to four children. Some families had up to six or seven. I was an only child for the first eleven years of my life. I lived in the same house as my three uncles, but they were a lot older. It just wasn't like having a brother. I used to fantasize about having a brother. I didn't think it would ever happen. My mother was in her late thirties and already had had a miscarriage. I was resigned to the fact that I would always be an only child.

We moved into our new house in April of 1959, courtesy of Anthony 'Spag' Borgatti. It was an exchange for our old house. A few months into our new home my mother informed me that she was going to have a baby. She also told me not to get too excited because of the last miscarriage.

As I saw her stomach getting larger with time, my anticipation grew. With her due date drawing closer, I realized it could happen! I could have a brother or sister! A sister would've been OK, but a brother! That was the ultimate.

It was a Saturday night when Mom started to get severe labor pains. I could feel the baby moving in her stomach. My father, feeling that time was near, had me sleep at my aunt's house.

Sunday morning, September 18, 1960, was a sunny day. My aunt and I walked briskly to the 9 a.m. Mass at St. Anne's Church. I knew Mom had gone to the hospital, but after having two close calls, I didn't hold out much hope this time either.

As the ending hymn was playing we slowly made our way out the back of the church. My aunt always bought the Sunday paper from the Telegram & Gazette vending box perched just outside. She'd always give me the quarter to get it. After paying, I quickly turned, with paper in hand, and caught up with my aunt, who, by this time, was quite a bit ahead of me.

While making our way down the long sidewalk toward Route 9, I saw what I thought was my uncle's '56 Nash going west on Route 9. Not thinking much of it, I waved and kept walking. At that point, my Uncle Emil, (or Chickie, as some people called him), yelled out the window the words I thought I'd never hear: "Helen had a baby boy!" I looked at my aunt, she looked at me, and we both hugged.

I couldn't believe it! I had a brother! I wasn't an only child anymore! A million thoughts raced through my head, but one had precedence over the others. He was going to be a baseball player. There were no ifs, ands, or buts about it. I could see it in my head. Little League, high school, college baseball, and maybe even the Major Leagues. I would make him eat, sleep, and drink baseball. It was in one instant, one of the happiest days an eleven year old can experience. I had my brother. My life was now complete.

It took my mother about two months to finally settle on a name for him. His first name is Joel, after Joel McCrea. His middle name is Donald, after my longtime friend, and now deceased, Donald Govoni.

As of this writing Joel or Jody, as we call him, is about to turn 56. After a great high school and college baseball career he was selected by the Cincinnati Reds in the baseball draft. Jody played baseball in Italy for six years. There, he met his wife Daniela. They have three children who speak perfect Italian. He is currently a Major League baseball scout for the Chicago White Sox and lives in Tampa, Florida.

As the years go on, I've had my own children and grandchildren, but I will never forget September 18, 1960. That was the day I finally became a brother.

25 Y.A. TITTLE, GIFFORD AND ROBUSTELLI

The New England, or Boston, Patriots came into existence in 1960, playing most of their games on Friday nights. As the Boston Patriots, they called many different stadiums home. Throughout the early to mid-'60s, they played at places such as Nickerson Field (Boston University), Boston College, and Fenway Park. They even played an exhibition game at Holy Cross' Fitton Field. As I said earlier, they played with a football that sported white lines three quarters of the way down on each end of the football.

This was Boston's entry into the newly formed American Football League. These players supposedly couldn't make the established National Football League. How could we get excited about them?

Our team was the New York Giants. These were the real football players who played in Yankee Stadium. They were players with the names Frank Gifford, Charley Connerly, Y. A. Tittle, Alex Webster, Rosie Grier, and Jim Catcavage. Every Sunday, almost everyone in New England watched the New York Giants on TV.

Back in the '50s and '60s, you couldn't buy an authentic game jersey for any sport, nor could you buy any authentic team equipment. It just wasn't sold in stores. My cousins and I had a plan. We'll take our plastic football helmets that we bought from Spag's, get some blue paint for the helmet, red paint for the stripe over the top of the helmet and white paint for the number sixteen that is split by the red line on the back of the helmet. Also in white is the New York team logo on both sides. The number 16 was for the Giants' running back

Frank Gifford. He was our favorite player.

When the Patriots moved into the newly built Schaefer Stadium and changed their name from Boston to New England, pretty much all of us became Patriots fans. But I'll always remember those great Giants teams with Sam Huff, Andy Robustelli, Gifford, and the rest.

26 LISTENING TO JOHNNY MOST

Growing up in a sports-minded family, I always had my athletic heroes. The first to come to mind are the obvious such as, Bill Russell, Bob Cousy, Ted Williams, and even John Havlicek. But one of my biggest heroes didn't even play a sport. It was Johnny Most, longtime broadcaster for the Boston Celtics.

In the '50s and early '60s we rarely, if ever, saw a Celtics game on television. Our only vision was what Johnny Most described on radio, and boy did he describe it. With his gravel voice and his staccato delivery, even though the game was on the radio, y o u c o u l d a l m o s t f e e l t h e a c t i o n o n t h e c o u r t. By J o h n n y ' s o w n admission, that voice was acquired from years of smoking too many cigarettes and drinking many cups of coffee.

To say Johnny Most was a homer would be an understatement. He was a homer in every sense of the word. When listening to one of his broadcasts, you would think the Celtics were the most victimized basketball team that ever played. As far as Johnny was concerned, the Celtics never committed a foul. Whichever team they were playing quickly became the villains.

Johnny would always start his broadcast by saying, "This is Johnny Most high above courtside where the Boston Celtics are getting ready to do basketball battle." Whenever play would get rough, he would emphatically state, "This game is taking on all the elements of a rock fight." When a player was trying to make a move toward the basket, Johnny would lightly say, "He tricky dribbles." If the player was dribbling for no reason, he would describe it by saying, "He fiddles, diddles and daddles." Jim Luscutoff stood 6'5" and carried 225 of solid muscle. Unlike the players of today who have full service weight rooms available, Luscy, as he was called, came by that build naturally.

Whenever Coach Arnold "Red" Auerback felt our players were pushed around or manhandled, in would come Luscutoff to straighten things out. Johnny Most would excitedly state, "Play is getting a little rough out there, here comes Jungle Jim," as he was affectionately called. "Watch out," Most would add. We would picture this muscular basketball player knocking the other team around and protecting our Celtics.

Undoubtedly his most famous call came in the seventh and final game of the league championship series against Wilt Chamberlain and the much hated Philadelphia 76ers. With a mere five seconds to play, Boston was leading by one point and had possession of the ball under the Philadelphia basket. Bill Russell was ready to inbound the pass, end the game and finish the series. Then the unthinkable happened.

As Russell was putting the ball in play, it somehow hit the guywire supporting the basket. Possession would now revert the 76ers. This was Johnny's call, "Russell is ---- he loses the ball off the support and Boston's only leading by one point!" All of us listening to the radio were thinking, *This can't be happening! We can't lose to Philly and Wilt! This just can't happen!* As my two cousins, my uncle, and I were listening, this was the way Johnny Most described it, "Greer getting ready to put the ball in play, he gets it out deep and Havlicek steals it, oh boy, Havlicek stole the ball, it's all over, it's all over, Johnny Havlicek stole the ball, it's all over! Believe that! Johnny Havlicek stole the ball! Bill Russell wants to hug John Havlicek, he squeezes John Havlicek. This, to me, was Johnny Most's signature call. It's readily available on YouTube. Every time I hear it, I feel like it's happening again. It still gives me goose bumps. After broadcasting Celtics games for almost 40 years, Johnny Most passed away in 1993. I don't listen to the Celtics on radio these days; to me, no announcer can ever compare to Johnny Most. In my mind I can still hear, "Sam Jones with the ball, tricky dribbles, puts up a 15-footer from right side, off the glass. Bang!"

Every broadcast would end with Johnny saying, "And so, Celtics fans, this is Johnny Most saying goodbye for now."

27 THE DAY THE '50s DIED

I've always felt the 1950s extended into the early '60s. Not much changed, at least in my life, from 1957-1963. It's true, I got a little older, slightly taller, but not much wiser. Men, women, and people of color still knew "their place." Baseball was king, and my mother still couldn't drive. That would all change on Friday afternoon, November 22, 1963.

I was just beginning to get used to the fact that I was now in high school, albeit the eighth grade. At that time it was the Shrewsbury Junior-Senior High School. We, as eighth graders, were packed on the lower level, or B Corridor, as it was known back then. I was looking forward to the upcoming basketball season and trying out for the junior varsity team. It was a fun time.

We were all told there would be a concert by the great violinist Rubinoff after lunch. I wasn't really up for that, but it was a Friday afternoon. The weekend beckoned. I guess I could put up with that, knowing that basketball tryouts would follow.

We filed into the auditorium and, being the youngest class, were seated in the front rows. As I sat waiting for the great violinist, one of the girls in class, sitting directly behind me, whispered to me that the President was shot, but I thought it was a joke. I responded by saying, "That's not something you joke about."

As we waited patiently, Rubinoff finally walked across the stage and immediately sat gingerly in a chair. He proceeded to open his violin case and promptly dropped something onto the stage floor. We laughed, he got mad. He then said, "If you laugh again I am leaving." After dropping another piece we laughed even louder. With that, Rubinoff stood up, called us the rudest bunch of people he'd ever met and quickly left the stage. Being high schoolers, we thought it was an act. But lo and behold, it wasn't. At that point Mr. Cooke, our principal, appeared on stage. He calmly stated, "Please excuse Mr. Rubinoff, he's had a rough day. Please file back to your homerooms and get ready for dismissal."

While we slowly made our way through the crowded hallways, rumors of an assassination started circulating throughout. Upon reaching my homeroom, my teacher, Mr. Vacca, was visibly shaken. His eyes were bloodshot red and his normally jovial attitude was sullen. As I peered into the eighth grade hallway, I could see small groupings of our teachers milling about. Some were crying and some displayed a look of shock on their faces. There was never any formal announcement, but just speculation over what happened in Dallas.

When the dismissal bell rang, I made my way to the gym. Remember, it was tryout day. Rumors abounded. President Kennedy had been shot, also Vice President Johnson and others. After a very short practice, I headed home. I had to find out the real story—all the time, in my mind, reassuring myself that this wasn't real. Maybe it was all a mistake. When I reached my house, I walked slowly through the garage and up the stairs. I can still see it as though it was yesterday.

My mother was ironing clothes in the kitchen. As our eyes met I asked her, "Is it true? Did it really happen?" She nodded "yes" and pointed to our 19-inch black and white television. I turned and looked at the image on the screen. It was the official portrait of President Kennedy with a black drape around it. The inscription at the bottom said, "President John F. Kennedy 1917-1963." Then it really hit me. He was gone! Our young, vibrant president was actually gone!

JFK was taken away from us at a very critical time in our young lives and it changed us profoundly. We looked at President Kennedy as a friend, not just a president. He was young. He even cracked jokes at his press conferences, which was unheard of at that time. Now he was gone.

In the days that followed, events became even more strange, but almost everyone living at that time can remember where they were or what they were doing the day the '50s died, November 22, 1963.

In retrospect, I believe that started the rebellion of young people in the '60s. It spawned the phrase, "Don't trust anyone over 30." The Beatles, with their moppy hair-dos, conquered our country. And, of course, there were the race riots of the late '60s.

Had that fateful day in Dallas not happened, would it have been a different country? I think so. We'll never know. I do know one thing. As an eighth grader, it changed my outlook on life forever. The only thing that didn't change was that my mother still couldn't drive.

CONCLUSION

This was the world as seen through the eyes of pre-teen growing up in Shrewsbury, Massachusetts, during the late '50s and early '60s. I'll leave it to you to decide if our lives are better today. Technology has certainly made life easier. I get into my air-conditioned car and play my pre-programmed music on my car stereo-radio. I have a cellphone that I carry all the time. I can log onto the computer and watch a boxing match between Rocky Marciano and Joe Walcott that took place 62 years ago. I can put soup in my microwave, and it'll be heated in seconds. I even have a camera that doesn't need film.

We have all this technology at our fingertips, yet are we any happier? I guess you'll have to answer that, but I really do like my remote electric car starter.

I think if we could incorporate the best of the '50s with the best parts of today, we would have one heck of a society.

POPULAR SPORTS STARS

Willie Mays Mickey
Mantle Rocky
Colavito Harmon
Killebrew Roger
Maris
Bob Cousy
Bill Russell
Frank Gifford
Y.A. Tittle
Eddie Mathews
Whitey Ford
Yogi Berra
Carl Yastrzemski
Duke Snider
Sandy Koufax
Hank Aaron
Frank Malzone
Wilt Chamberlain
Jerry West

POPULAR TV SHOWS

The Honeymooners

Amos 'n' Andy

Your Show of Shows

Gillette Cavalcade of Sports Beat the Clock

I Love Lucy

The Lone Ranger

The Adventures of Superman

The Howdy Doody Show

Ding Dong School

The Life of Riley

Sky King Fury

The Roy Rogers Show

Hopalong Cassidy

The Cisco Kid

The Range Rider

Sugarfoot Wagon

Train Wyatt Earp

Cheyenne

Gunsmoke

Captain Kangaroo

Jack Lalanne

Highway Patrol

The Jack Paar Show

The Mickey Mouse Club

Boomtown

The Arthur Godfrey Show

The Today Show

The Phil Silvers Show

The Real McCoys

Zorro

Leave it to Beaver

The Ed Sullivan Show

SGT Preston of the Yukon

Dick Van Dyke Show

Bonanza

The Rifleman

The Andy Griffith Show

Batman

The Munsters

The Adams Family

The Beverly Hillbillies

Petticoat Junction

Judge Roy Bean

Yancy Derringer

The Price is Right

Concentration

The Millionaire

The Art Linkletter Show

Car 54

Combat

Topper

The Big Valley

Mister Ed

McHale's Navy

Henry Grampietro

Gilligan's Island

My Three Sons

ABC's Wide World of Sports

Dennis the Menace

Ball Parks

Fenway Park – Boston, MA

Crosley Field – Cincinnati, OH

Municipal Stadium – Kansas City, KS

Comiskey Park – Chicago, IL

County Stadium – Milwaukee, WI

Briggs Stadium – Detroit, MI

Forbes Field – Pittsburg, PA

Yankee Stadium – New York City, NY

Sportsmans Park – Washington DC

Los Angeles Coliseum – Los Angeles, CA

Memorial Stadium – Baltimore, MD

Seals Stadium – San Francisco, CA

Polo Grounds – New York City, NY

ABOUT THE AUTHOR

Henry Grampietro is a life long resident of Shrewsbury, MA, graduate of Shrewsbury High School Class of 1968. Also, graduate of Quinsigamond Community College, Worcester State College with a Bachelor of Arts degree in Education. Owner of Grampietro Photography a portrait and wedding business. Currently a substitute teacher at Shrewsbury High School.

Made in the USA
Columbia, SC
30 June 2018